CANDLE IN THE DARK

A POSTSCRIPT
TO DESPAIR

CANDLE
IN THE DARK

*A POSTSCRIPT
TO DESPAIR*

By

IRWIN EDMAN

JONATHAN CAPE
THIRTY BEDFORD SQUARE
LONDON

FIRST PUBLISHED, 1940

JONATHAN CAPE LTD. 30 BEDFORD SQUARE, LONDON
AND 91 WELLINGTON STREET WEST, TORONTO

PRINTED IN GREAT BRITAIN BY BUTLER AND TANNER LTD.
FROME AND LONDON
PAPER SUPPLIED BY SPALDING AND HODGE LTD.
BOUND BY A. W. BAIN AND CO. LTD.

To
J. B. GOLD
in memory
of
days of peace

CANDLE IN THE DARK

'*A shipwrecked sailor on this coast*
bids you set sail,
Full many a gallant ship ere we were lost
weathered the gale.'

CANDLE IN THE DARK

A POSTSCRIPT TO
DESPAIR

THE faiths by which men live are various, and some, like love, happiness, progress, and success, may hardly be recognized as faiths at all. But they are beliefs, and men act on them. To sensitive human beings everywhere the most serious of casualties has already come. That casualty is the collapse of everything by which the hopeful spirit or the generous mind has lived. For the second time in a generation the brutal futility of war has broken out in the very heart of the civilized world, in lands that are the sources of ourselves and our culture. Whatever be the causes, whatever the necessity, the fact that there could be such causes and such necessity has already eaten like a canker into the bloom of every value we enjoy and every ideal we cherish. It has seemed to make a mockery of all our hopes, and non-sense of all our knowledge. It has turned the faith in education into an irony and has reduced to triviality the arts on which men have lavished their technical mastery and their lyric flame. It has made even private joys seem precarious and shamefaced. What do all these things avail, when they end in deliberate death and incalculable chaos? Men in the nineteenth century were sad that they could no longer believe in God. They are more deeply saddened now by the fact that they can no longer believe in man.

What, in the face of such overwhelming collapse, is there for us to escape to or to cling to or to lean on? Where may we turn, in Æ.'s wonderful phrases, from 'the politics of time' to 'the politics of eternity'?

What can we do to keep sane in a world gone mad?

*

For it is impossible to ignore so universal a disaster. Even the Ivory Tower is not bombproof, nor can we retreat into ourselves, for our deepest thoughts and sentiments are coloured by a world catastrophe. Like it or not, we must think and we must feel about it. For once in our lives we are compelled to concern ourselves about issues larger than ourselves and about interests not immediately our own.

So it comes about, strangely, at a time when action is most virulent, when conditions are most violent in the world, that we are compelled to turn to thoughts apparently remote, to raise fundamental issues, and to ask fundamental questions. If all the goods of life are uncertain, we are harried into asking what the goods of life really are. If all our expectations have been defrauded, we are led to ask what the proper expectations of man may be.

If our science is rendered suspect because of the horror it produces or the happiness it has failed to produce, we are driven to consider the real hope and scope of science. If our education is futile, we necessarily ask what kind of education might not be. If our art is trivial, we must inquire what would constitute a major or healing art. In a time of despair we are driven to philosophy, which may, as somebody once called it, be at least 'a dim candle over a dark abyss'. Unless we are to go, like the continent of Europe, completely to pieces, we must turn to some organic and unifying consideration of life. In so turning we shall re-assess even our despair and possibly be rescued from some of our disillusionment. If we do not find a solution, we may, in the very act of thinking, find an unexpected ano-dyne, for fundamental thinking involves the past, the future, and the timeless. Some, at least, of the sting of the present is removed, for even the present is seen at arm's length.

The first temptation is to escape into a

vague mysticism or a definite callousness. But if we were really callous we could not be so deeply hurt. It is because we are not insensible that we turn to escape in brisk and cynical hardness; where tomorrows are all dark, it seems reasonable to live for the day. Or (it happened during the last war) we turn to vague mysticism, to philosophies that tell us that, though all is apparent chaos, there are reason and beauty at the core. We are not children. We cannot thus fool ourselves. For many, still, there is comfort in the thought that God moves in a mysterious way his wonders to perform. But for the rest of us?

There is an old Arabic proverb: 'Hope is a slave, despair a free man.' Surely in that sense today we are all free. But despair itself is one of the things we must re-examine. Perhaps we are despairing because we had hoped too much or in the wrong direction. If we are desperate, what are we desperate about?

Our unhappiness has a longer history than the outbreak of war, our horror is not simply the desolation and the destruction

13

of war, ruined cities in Poland, and millions again mobilized on the Western Front. It is a terror, growing in the hearts of men ever since 1914, not only that the values for which men live are in danger but that the very principles by which they live are being rendered null. We despair that ever again will the glory and beauty of the civilized world be enjoyed by free men in spiritual or even physical security.

For though men have felt guilt about their enjoyment of the world, they have enjoyed it. Though Truth, Goodness, and Beauty have been hard to define, men have died for them or lived by them. Now truth is publicly flouted in the major decisions that affect all mankind. An almost diabolical unconcern for human feelings, for human suffering or human happiness, seems to be the central creed of powerful people on whose decisions depend unnumbered instances of private well-being. Not only is the creation of beauty interrupted, but the subtle pursuit of its distinctions, the fine attunement required for its enjoyment, seem to have no place and no function. And what is worse, there is no guarantee that men will have them again after all this is over. Name, one by one, things for which men care or by which they live — private affections, simple physical pleasures, public good, common arts, large and liberating ideas, the primary decencies or the ultimate values — they are either threatened or sidetracked or made suspect.

It is one of the major tragedies of the present tragic time that this should be so. For, in an important sense, nothing has been changed, though everything has been interrupted. One would not go on listening to Beethoven if one's house were afire, but the beauty of music remains no less beautiful because our listening to it must be postponed. If the world is going to smash, one's personal ambitions or one's griefs or loves seem relatively unimportant. But no amount of the regimentation of war erases the fact that ultimately public welfare becomes actual in the private joys of single individuals. The common welfare is the well-being of individual men.

Nothing has changed. But everything has a new and desolating context.

For the fact of a war involving economically and morally the whole of civilization has put every other fact before us in a strange and sombre light. It is impossible to enjoy even the simplest of daily experiences without remembering. Amid the reds of the peaceful Connecticut autumn one thinks of foreign battlefields and blood. In the brilliant dusk of an October day along the Hudson one is reminded of soldiers massed at the Vistula or by the Rhine. In the snug companionship of families and friends, one recalls how many families are broken up, and how many friends separated, perhaps for ever.

Doubt enters the very citadel of our enjoyments and devotions. Embarrassment, almost a sense of guilt, infects the normal casualness and gaiety of conversation in our own living-rooms and with our familiars. We can have serenity of mind, if at all, only if we divest ourselves of all our comfortable illusions, and gaze candidly on whatever bare moral minimum we have left. We must face the fact that the faith of the modern man, to whatever low level it has receded, must recede still further before it can rise again. For it is not only the grand commitments of hopes that are rendered bankrupt; it is also the narrower, less pretentious, more personal assumptions. Along with faith in the whole of humanity must vanish reliance, for a sense of well-being, on private pleasure and success. Private pleasure has become tainted and personal success both empty and uncertain. A disaster so wide reaches into every nook of soliloquy and corrupts the most modest personal joy. How long we can know these, even the most fortunate of us, we are not certain, and to even the most callous it has occurred and recurred that in a world so awry we have no right to enjoy them at all, or we find, if we think we have the right, that the joy has been poisoned at the heart.

In the present war as in the last one, in the next dubious peace as in the last, it is not unnatural that we should look for consolation in some facet of the fact of war itself. War, much as we hate to admit it, gives, even for us not in the midst of it, a sudden edged preciousness to values we had taken for granted, like light when night is falling, or conversation with a friend one knows is doomed to die. 'The blackberries are almost ripe', an English friend wrote me the day after war had begun, and he on the eve of war service, 'and I almost deliberately enjoy the gardening today.' The day becomes poignantly beautiful in a setting autumn sun. The very tameness of our usual easy pleasures acquires a wild flush of beauty when they are dislocated or threatened. The normal becomes abnormally interesting. And the abnormality of war itself, seen at a distance by the neutral civilian, becomes a tragic spectacle. We live, it is borne in upon us, in the midst of great issues. In point of fact, we always do, but in time of a war involving a great part of the civilized nations of the world, those issues become sharpened in outline; as at a tragedy we are the fascinated participants in a vital battle; all our private irresolutions are overshadowed by the tensions of the decision to be made: we are exalted by the dubious arbitrament of blood. The actual pain, misery, and boredom of the war for those involved in it are, for some at least, balanced by the perverse excitement of hates that have an object, and crusades that have a point. There is no time for moaning about futility, though the last war proved to have been futile.

The chaos of events has a specious meaning once the conflict is afoot. Even for those not among the nations involved, the tensions are real, the occasion large, the wine for imagination heady. It was repeatedly remarked after the last war how great a let-down and a laxness of feeling occurred directly the war was over. When the fighting stopped, the peace was empty, for during the four years the very interruption of peace had given a temporary significance to life and society. The thunder of guns drowned out all other meaning or the absence of all other meaning. During a great war the little pleasures seem bigger; the bigger doubts temporarily are forgotten. For the time being we lose the power of mind save for one end. Private depressions seem puny, and cosmic pessimism remote.

Then again, by one of the strange psychoses of the war temper, for once the moral loneliness and isolation of individuals seem to be transcended. Even when they disagree about the aim of war, or the hopes for peace, it is for once a common theme that individuals are largely thinking about or haunted by. Their thinking is focused on a universally intelligible fact, though, or because, it is a terrible one. There is probably no other time in the complexities of the modern world when this is true. It is ironic but significant that only when all the concerns of humanity are threatened is the common humanity of man present to the minds of all. It is not until the boat is sinking that we are made to realize that we are in the same boat. During a common crisis there is a frightened closeness of human association. In a dark time men for once realize that they are brothers in desperation.

And in that dark time, another common bond arises. 'I am too busy to think,' my English friend wrote in the letter quoted above, 'but when I do I cannot help wondering what sort of world may be patched up after all this is over.' So does everyone. The worst war cannot go on for ever, and the resilience of life is such that to live at all it is imperative to look beyond the darkness to a possible light. Already we are thinking of what kind of world it may be 'after all this is over'. *The world after the war.* The words become an ironic emptiness to those of us who lived through the last one. For this *is* the world after the war, this very present, war-dazed world we are in. In the last war, too, the quality of the moment became precious. In the last war, too, men had common aims or felt a common tragedy. During the last war, too, men planned for a better society in the peace to come. And we know now how rapidly, once the war is over, these things pass: the comfort intensified by danger, the common bond provided by a universal calamity, the gleam shining bravely in the darkness.

All these things we recognize now, yet (or else we could not live at all) our impulse and obligations keep us going. We breathe, we eat, we love. No hostilities can put a moratorium on these instinctive assertions of life. Our work is continued out of habit, and our economic need for work remains in war as in peace. But in war as in peace there is some time to think, and a war prompts us more than is usual with us to think about ultimate matters. And when we do think, we discover the depths of the disaster that has overtaken us. For we are assailed by a tormenting uneasiness about both the usual furniture of our existence — our pleasures, our comforts, and our security — and the principles by which almost instinctively we had lived. The things we love and the ideas we live by have been brutally challenged or exploded.

First as to the things we have taken for

granted as normal. Psychiatry has of late made us self-conscious and dubious about human virtue, it is true. But there is for most people, I think, the residual sense that, whatever misery there may be in life, whatever sliminess in persons, on the whole, a certain measure of comfort and enjoyment is the normal part of life and a certain measure of decency, courtesy, and companionability may be assumed to animate human beings and control their behaviour. The outbreak of war has merely brought to a focus our suspicion that a relatively pleasant life and a relatively decent behaviour are not the standard equipment and the standard practice of human beings. Even in times of 'peace', peace has been shattered by news whose horror is not less because for years we have had to be accustomed to it. We do not need news of tortures practised on a large scale in concentration camps or in Chinese battles. In times of tranquillity at home there are scenes of violence and misery from which we are compelled, or compel ourselves, to avert our eyes. Life is, we hardly need to be reminded, not marked by the smooth security of the middle class. The standards of comfortable and pleasant living have never been universal. A war merely dramatically destroys them in fact or in spirit for us all. Pain and violence, death and frustration, become a patent spectacle for all mankind and an unavoidable experience for a good part of it. In times of peace we could at least hope that the friendly ease possible for the comfortable classes might, if sufficient wit and good will contrived it, be possible for everyone. But we now see how thin, ineffective, and limited are the operations of courtesy and comfort and friendliness, how restricted the sphere in which gaiety and enjoyment obtain. What is the use of being told to cultivate our garden, when bombshells may land in its midst, or when we know what sadness lies over the garden wall?

Then, too, the gently bred and reasonably instructed have long felt that education in sensibility and reason might make good will and good sense prevail. For most

24

liberal-minded people had in the past hundred years gone to the opposite extreme from the dire theological estimate of unregenerate human nature. Even the widespread popularity of psychoanalysis had not cured us of a fairly genial estimate of human nature and the possibilities that lay in its education. Psychiatry, it is true, had revealed how much of the animal and the savage lay embedded in our subconscious, but until the recent spread of barbarism and violence over Europe and the Orient most liberal minds had been prepared to excuse our vices on the grounds of the burden of bestiality and chaos that lay within our psyches. For the most part, with the gradual growth of humanitarian sentiment and activity through the nineteenth century, it seemed not impossible to believe that a certain kind of decency and harmony, the sort of behaviour that people exhibited toward one another when they were not 'too unhappy to be kind', might gradually come to control large human affairs. Briand could say triumphantly after one of those hopeful between-war conferences at which he and Stresemann had learned to understand each other, 'We speak not as Frenchmen or Germans, but as Europeans.' English boys went tramping through the countryside, and lodging in the youth hostels, of Germany, and one envisaged a future when men might all really speak with the accents of humanity.

Psychiatry had long made us suspicious, and fanaticism on a nation-wide scale has now made us completely despair of any such humane future. The democratic hypothesis, which is essentially the belief in the self-improvability of humanity, has not seemed to work, and neither has the technical mastery of science on which it is based. Faith in the perfectibility of human nature and, through human nature, of human institutions has suffered a severe setback. The chances of implementing good will with a good life seem slim. We have lost our faith in the common hopes of the common man and the human wisdom of the ingenious and the learned. There has probably never been a time when the faith in democracy, however we may still cherish it, has been at a lower ebb; never a period when the human benefits of science or its promise of felicity has been more completely called into question.

*

The faith in science ought perhaps to be examined first, for it was on scientific method, until a quarter of a century ago, that we had banked most of our hopes. The most painful part of the irony lies in the fact that in one respect there is nothing to disillusion us — within certain limits, our reliance upon scientific method has been more than justified. Increasingly it has appeared that there is almost nothing that men cannot accomplish in their mastery over things. There is nothing that men cannot do, but there seems almost nothing too terrible for which they will not use or cannot be made to use their unprecedented powers. The science that was to make life beautiful has also made it hideous. It rains bombs upon defenceless cities as well as celestial music upon enraptured ears. It invents unspeakable tortures as well as the clean beauties of modern architecture. It brings the most elegant and disciplined of chamber music into our homes but it carries thereto also the voices of the demagogue and the dictator. It gives us abundance but has not prevented starvation in the midst of plenty. It gives us longer life — and swifter death. We are able to accomplish incredible transformations of incalculable resources and to achieve everything except security and peace. Surgery marvellously salvages men shattered by an equally marvellous precision. Fields of grain and flocks of sheep are destroyed while gifted chemists devise substitutes for bread and wool. The same infinite capacity that might change and improve the world is used to destroy it.

The faith in political democracy has suffered no less than the faith in scientific method. Before the first World War the liberal mind could look forward to the day when co-operative intelligence nourished by universal education could make the world a family of nations and individuals members of a national family. The lion and the lamb of labour and capital, prophets such as H. G. Wells used to assure us, were to lie down together, and nations, races, and creeds were to live in a friendly atmosphere of universal good will. That dream of corporate world-wide felicity has vanished at the very time that rapid communication and world-wide technology were making the planet small in scope and one in its involvements. Representative government has not been able to provide at once for the comforts and for the security of a people, and to maintain, untampered with, the individual variety of their lives. Nor has representative government turned out to be representative of any but the economically dominant interests. Part of the 'revolt of the masses', ironically betrayed in Russia and betrayed from the outset in Germany, came from the fact that democracy did not work as a true democracy, nor was the pluto-oligarchy that passed for democracy able to function; in a contracting world economy, with both internal breakdown and imperialistic clashes, these pseudo-democracies came to grief. September 1939 was the climactic date of our disillusion, but it had been twenty years a-growing.

No wonder we speak of the failure of the laboratory, and the bankruptcy of democracy. We have with purely human intelligence achieved marvels of superhuman technical cunning. But we have not had enough combined beneficent cunning to turn the world from a twenty years' threat of a shambles into a garden home of quiet, individual pleasure and shared joy.

★

But the deepest cause for doubt is not the failure of specific principles, for such failures are natural enough in a world where all life is a risk and where intelligence is an adventure. It is the failure of that principle by which all principles are corrected. It is the slavery of principles, racial, national, cultural, philosophical, that is part of the source of our disasters. Absolutes in ideas turn into fanaticisms in action; principles we are willing to die for may also become, if we live by them, a death in life. We are not driven to melancholy because reason has erred. We may think with Socrates that if reasoners err, it is not reason that is at fault. Our chagrin comes not from the fact that we are compelled to re-examine our principles, but from the fact that we are suspicious of the capacity to be intelligently self-critical, when intelligence has made such an apparently hopeless muddle of its affairs. Our bafflement comes rather from the fact, even more desolating, that though there is evident and current any amount of reasonableness among a relatively small group of men, enlightenment, reasonableness, the habit of criticism, along with amiability and decency of behaviour, seem utterly no match for ruthless power and brutal domination. The bass notes of unreason have made reason itself, such of it as remains, a very thin treble in the affairs of men.

It is thus not the setback of principles, of belief in democracy, or in human nature, or in the goods of life, that has been most devastating. The discovery that principles are wrong, that practices are ineffective, would not trouble us so deeply. What does give us pause is that the instrument on which liberal hopes had above all relied, the instrument of reason itself, has been revealed as so tiny a flicker, so negligible a force, in the governance of mankind. If we carry within us a burden of childishness, savagery, and animality, the same psychiatric science that had taught us to recognize those gave us also the hope that we might in time learn to direct them. The same realism that pointed out the difficulties inherent in the practice of democracy could also promise us a technique for overcoming those difficulties.

We have come, I think, for the first time since the early nineteenth century, to the point where, especially among progressive minds, the deep fear has arisen that intelligence itself is pathetically ineffective. For, against all those convenient shibboleths of nineteenth-century hopefulness, comes the stark assertion of force. Fanaticism is in the saddle. Brute power is dominant in civilization, and things have come indeed to such a pass that the very nations which condemn such an assertion of power find that only by brute resistance can brute power itself be repulsed. Good will and good sense indeed! The climax of our disillusion comes in the fact that civilized virtues appear to have no place and no jurisdiction in a world where ill-will and madness prevail.

★

The world of tomorrow! When we can scarcely bear to consider what may follow from the world of today! No wonder, therefore, that, despairing of what man has made and seems to be making of the present, there has grown up all over Europe and America a nostalgia for the past. There has been a deep-seated tendency to look elsewhere than at the present, a tendency that the last catastrophic turn of events will enhance. We shall continue to have, as we have been having these last years, nostalgic memoirs, backward looks to a simpler, more stable society. The sentimental backward glance has been very popular in the last twenty years. The past is smoothed out; we are given everything but the pain and death and squalor, and even when given these, at a distance, they are aureoled in sentiment as pain, death, and squalor are not aureoled in the screaming actuality of the present. When we are desperate enough, Utopia comes to lie in the day before yesterday. Vienna is in the hands of ruthless conquerors, but we can turn, in imagination at least, to the Vienna of waltzes and wines, of gaiety, of kindliness, of German feeling with a French accent and a French *élan*. There are sandbags in the streets of London, and London at night is a medieval city without lights and with the fear of sudden death in the dark from on high. It is excusable enough if we turn to dreams of the England of Thackeray and Dickens, of a settled social order, of Christmas jollity even among the poor, of untroubled elegance among the rich, of cricket games on village greens, of bracing walks on wind-swept moorlands with no threatening hum of aircraft overhead. It is natural that in New York, amid the tensions of a seaport visited by armed mer-chantmen and refugees arriving from nerve-racked cities in the theatre of war, we retreat in fancy to a little older New York, where people knew their neigh-bours, and the city was a small town of friends. Now, more than ever, we are tempted to escape to a world of horse-and-buggy doctors, of village stage coaches, of crinolines, of guitars sounding on June nights on plantation verandas, to a period of simple homely virtues, of the old-fashioned American way.

It is natural enough that the flight to yesterday should occur when today is almost unbearable. We turn to the past when the future looks terrifying or looks blank. Then, most of all, the Golden Age is identified with the Garden of Eden; Heaven is not to be gained or even regained; felicity is Paradise Lost. The Garden of Eden is our childhood, or, since if we are honest we remember some painful moments there, the childhood of our grandparents, where, we like to believe, there were no wars or rumours of wars, or only very little ones. Forgetting the Caesars and Napoleons, we forget too that there were dictators and, ignoring the history books, that there were battles or conquests. We envy Thoreau meditating by Walden Pond, Emerson conversing on high matters with pure spirits in Concord, or the family group in *Little Women*, forgetting too that that idyll took place with the American Civil War going on. 'Once upon a time' means once upon a better time, where all tales ended happily, when evil was but a transient shadow to vanish or be conquered by the good.

Doubtless now that the present is so

bleak and the future so ominous we shall more than ever turn to the past. But not without misgivings. For almost everyone now is inclined to suspect that it is only the urgency of the present that makes the past seem so desirable. Our picture of the past is a present with the blemishes removed, put a thousand years ago or yesterday. But we are here, it is now; whatever peace of mind we attain must be based upon that incorrigible recognition.

★

In previous ages when external events were too terrifying or too hopeless, men could retreat into themselves. They could face the alien world with a certain equanimity, safe and serene so long as they breathed in the solace and the rectitude, the generosity and the courage, of their own ideals.

It was partly out of despair, personal and social, that W. E. Henley could write:

It matters not how strait the gate,
  How charged with punishments the
    scroll,
I am the master of my fate:
  I am the captain of my soul.

We have seen any number of tragic evidences these past years of how much brave, foolish rhetoric is involved in those lines. The bravest of spirits is not the master of his fate when he is in a concentration camp under brutal guards. Nor is it easy to be the captain of one's soul when the captain is confused and doubts whether he is the captain, when his course is not clear and he wonders whether the ports he is headed for are worth making, or can be made before he sinks.

Even apart from external circumstances, the internal weather of our souls has been cloudy these last fateful years. Darker than any outer darkness is what St. John of the Cross called the dark night of the soul. The psychiatrists have made us suspicious of our ideals and our motives, and the economists and the sociologists have rendered us uneasy as to the sources of what we hold most dear. Sex and money are not only at the root of all evil, but of all good. We come trailing clouds, not of glory, but of greed and lust. The outer world with its spread of barbarism simply confirms our worst thoughts about ourselves; it takes away the sacred citadel of ourselves, too. Without too great a conviction of sin, we may still feel that the picture of life today in the world is simply the expression of the childishness, the savagery, the animality which we have of late discovered about ourselves. The inner world as well as the outer one is barbarism. The inner prospect is no nobler than the external one. The latter is the evil in man's soul become an epidemic in the world. Or the soul of man, as the psychiatrists reveal it to us, is simply the state of society reflected, as in an exact mirror, in ourselves.

*

In times of despair in the past, men have been able to retire into something deeper than themselves. Saints and mystics have recommended the serenity that might be attained if only one could be sufficiently still. If the outer world were steadfastly disregarded, if the inner tumult were sufficiently subdued, within the collected psyche something solacing and deep would sound. In the depths of one's own retired being, all Being would speak; one would be at peace with the eternal. The tumult without is now too loud; the conflict and doubt within are too strong. Part of our desolation comes from the fact that there are no collected silent spaces for the spirit. It is part of our tragedy that the rapt quiet of the saints and mystics, the collected sanctuary of the spirit, is not possible for us in these agitating times. Not in the self, nor in the past, nor in a mystical absorption, is escape to be found, and the present seems to offer no ground for hope. It is, as Bertrand Russell once put it, 'on the firm foundation of unyielding despair that the soul's habitation henceforth alone can be safely built'. Any comfort we can find must be a postscript to despair.

Only when we are willing to call into question everything we have taken for granted, only on the precarious bedrock of doubt, can we rise to any encouragements, or can any consolations be found. What brief candles of hope or of resource can we find in a darkness which we are first prepared to accept as absolute? What, amid the noisy alarms and scarring disillusions, can the mind remaining at once candid and liberal hope for?

*

The first ray of hope, perhaps, lies in the discovery that the darkness may be not so absolute as we had supposed. Nihilism is a form of hysteria, and hysteria occurs where the patient, having no possible solution, moans incoherently in confused defeat. Bad as the present is, it seems worse than any past only by virtue of the fact that it has its sharp edge of being here and now. This is, of course, not the first time in the history of civilization that sensitive spirits, bred in a familiar culture, have declared,

41

because that culture was changing, that all civilization was coming to an end.

This is not the first time in the history of the West that the good and the reasonable saw nothing to do but to die or to shudder. It is sobering to our too hysterical fears to take, under the guidance of competent historians, a historical perspective. It requires a hard, even a cruel effort at detachment to take the long view, but only by taking such a view can we see our present plight in something like its true proportions and find true proportions for our still persistent hopes. We shall, by so doing, discover that part of the nihilism that is in the air is the result of a strange — and absurd — conviction that we are living in a new kind of present, one without a past and without a future. Men in earlier ages, too, thought they were living at the end of the world. Nothing comes out of nothing, Lucretius once long ago informed his readers. No civilization ever ends. Let us calm ourselves a little by citing the words of an eminent historian of the Middle Ages:

'The Middle Ages can be rightly under-
stood only as a period of convalescence,
slow at best, and with continual relapses,
from the worst catastrophe recorded in the
whole history of the Western World. . . .
The break-up of the [Roman] Empire was
followed by scenes of disorder, not only far
more intense than what we have seen in
the most unhappy districts of modern
times, but prolonged for a period exceed-
ing the worst that we can possibly fear as
a result of the present international rivalries and class conflicts. . . . Generations
later, when the barbarians had burst in
and Alaric the Goth had even taken
Rome, men felt as though the sky had
fallen.' (Coulton, *Medieval Panorama*, pp.
8–9.)

The sky had not fallen; it never has done
so; it never will. There is every evidence
that the civilization of Western Europe as
we men have known it for hundreds of
years is in eclipse, in the sense that forces
are coming to birth that will make it in-
conceivably different. What would Western culture be like without our familiar

religions, arts, and aspirations? So much of our imaginative heritage is bound up with that world that radical changes in it seem very like an end, and that end very like a tragedy. But though the Roman Empire collapsed, the elements of civilization it contained have survived. And if a complicated and decaying system of politics, finance, and privilege, blended with religion, is now passing away, that does not mean that all the past values it has enshrined are ended, or that they will not come to life again in a freer and more equitable world. The glory that was Greece continued to live in the grandeur that was Rome, and Rome endures today in our thoughts, emotions, our institutions and arts, in our laws and our languages. St. Augustine said the City of God lives on for ever while the empires of man pass away. But all that counts in the City of Man, too, has survived; only the imperial matrix has vanished. Civilizations do not end; they change, and terrible as are the crises and disorders through which Western civilization has passed, it has never altogether ceased. We are too nihilistic. We prematurely and provincially assume that, because the present bodes an end to established empires, it is the end of all things. The world seemed to a good many Athenians, too, to have ended with the Peloponnesian War.

Historical-mindedness may rescue us, then, from the sense that we are living in a twilight of the gods. Perhaps our gods were not all gods, perhaps new gods are being born. But it may be argued that only from the point of view of astronomical coolness or geological leisure can one speak so calmly of the lapse of a civilization with which all the moral and æsthetic and practical interests of contemporary lives are concerned. Nor can the actuality of present agonies be brushed away in such grandiose detachment. But to remember the past, to be historical-minded, if it does not give us too great expectations, at least removes us from a hysterical piling up of our worst fears and an exacerbated awareness of evil. We read of casualties by the thousand in unde-

45

clared wars in the Orient and of the tensions of the theatre of war now closer to home in the West, of executions by the score in countries at peace, of starvation in lands of abundance. We ask, could anything at any time have been worse? The answer is that they could have been and that they have been. The collapse of the Roman Empire is not simply a graph in a later historian's pages. It meant actual painful disorder in the lives of millions of men for hundreds of years. Much later, the Thirty Years' War was one of the worst scourges, one of the most terrible and futile ravagings of European civilization, in recorded history. The news of it did not spread in hectic flashes instantly over the whole of mankind. But it was quite as acutely damaging to innocent and helpless individuals as anything men suffer today. The Thirty Years' War was but one among many times when the generous and reasonable could only lament and despair, if they were not themselves in too dire distress to look at that of others with either detachment or sympathy. It is not,

I think, sentimentalism to point out that men have survived — certainly cultures and nations and races have survived — other crises, worse crises than even that of the national rivalries and class conflicts of today. It is true that the miseries of our own time are no less acute, its terrors no less frightening, because other ages had their share. But we need to be reminded of the epitaph of the shipwrecked sailor quoted in the Greek anthology:

A shipwrecked sailor on this coast bids you
    set sail,
Full many a gallant ship ere we were lost
    weathered the gale.

Our own tragedies are acutely our own, but they are not final in the universe, nor do they preclude a renascence of life in perhaps more liberal and intelligent forms. Vegetation dies every autumn, but Nature does not die. So, too, with forms of human living. There will be springs again, and even now children are being born whose adult lives will begin when the storm is over, and when they may have learned to build better than we. And if the houses of their spirit have a different architecture, they may be no less beautiful; they may well be more solid and more roomy than our own inherited forms of shelter, and to the generations who will live in them quite as homely and familiar and as much the stimulus to affection and imagination as anything we have known.

But historical-mindedness has other uses than to show us that things were once worse or just as bad or just as portentous — or that Nature generates new ways of life for men. Its real uses are to show us the roots and sources of our worst evils and in the very revelation of their origins show us hints of their possible cures. This civilization itself, which we moan to see in collapse, contained, obviously, the very disease which produced the present crisis. We will not be quite so benumbed by the disaster if we see its long-range sources; we shall feel less a collectively suicidal impulse. Willy-nilly, we shall go on having expectations, for to live at all is to expect, but our hopes will be more sober and less treacherous. Historical-mindedness is important above all in giving us the habit of thinking in terms of causes and consequences. We shall see that, if not all our expectations were sober, neither were all our despairs. Why should we, in the long historical perspective, despair of science, democracy, and human nature itself?

★

On the negative side, even the most bitter admit that physical science has been a triumphant and, as in the diabolical new technique of high explosives, sometimes a grimly spectacular success. So much have the miracles of the technique of physical science become familiar that they are banal. But we need to be reminded again how young a venture is scientific method and how limited the fields in which it has been tried. The present state to which civilization has come is not a cue to give up the hope of improvement of mankind through understanding. Rather it is brought home to us tragically to what a pass we are come when we leave human relations, private and public, to the devices of vested interests, fanatic formulas, and uninstructed passions. Small as is the area in which intelligence has been applied to social and human problems, it has been strikingly effective. Psychiatry is, in the modern sense, simply a child, yet it has begun to remake the souls of men. Where economic opportunity and stability have permitted it, education, too, for all its failures, has made thousands upon thousands of children — born, like children in any age, little bundles of animal savagery — into reasonable and decent human beings. Even in this disordered society there are thousands upon thousands of instances of relatively ordered and sometimes beautiful lives. Scientific method is simply a name for the technique of human art applied to human problems. There is nothing but a challenge in the fact that the social and moral scene is still in chaos and threatens to be in worse disorder before it improves.

There is even a kind of encouragement in our recognition of just how much the war is interrupting the beneficent arts of healing, of teaching, and of housing and communication. No one can have seen Europe in the past twenty years without noting in how many directions, even under the constant threat of war, new and fruitful methods in education, in socialized medicine, in methods of social security have been developed. It was in Vienna, starving and uneasy, that some of the finest schemes of workers' housing grew. Even in the maelstrom of insecurity that we now see the Weimar Republic to have been, youth movements, modern building, and a lively folk theatre were being encouraged. In the Scandinavian countries, as many recent books have reminded us, intelligence (a simpler name for scientific method) was making the pattern of a rich shared life, of a simple, sensible culture in which it was possible for all to have a part without acrimony. In this world, what-

ever bruises and disruptions, whatever
sore spots of sweated workers and dis-
tressed areas there may be (all symptoms
of the failure of intelligence), there has
been in every direction the remaking of
life, ranging from garden cities and parks
to enlightened child guidance — indica-
tions of what technique combined with
good will may make of our society.

That there is much to be done remains
unquestioned; that there is much now seriously threatened no one in his senses could
deny. But even under the dislocations of
the past twenty years, now seen as a mere
truce between wars, what *has* been done
indicates what can be done. It is nothing
less than hysteria or failure of nerve to
believe that all is over because everything
is interrupted. Indeed it would seem part
of the very minimum of moral sanity
today to keep in mind firmly that, however tragic and far-reaching the interregnum through which we are passing, it
is an interregnum, even in Europe. It is to
become a partner in the current madness
that has overtaken the world to abet the

madness by an abdication of just those interests and activities which in the long perspective make for the world's sanity. Nothing that matters in an ordered time matters less now. The schools, the medicine, the research, the co-operative inquiry that are the only instruments of a better-ordered world are now more critically important than ever. It is not callousness but concern for the future of men that should urge us to keep alive the only enterprise working toward a more rational and equitable society. There is a parable in the story of Fray Luis Ponce de Léon, long ago imprisoned for his political opinions, who returned after seven years to his class at the university and began, 'As I was saying.' Whatever men were saying or doing that made sense or was fruitful in life and society is no less sensible and fruitful now. It will not be less sensible or fruitful after the war is over. There is a chance, a bare chance, of course, that Europe will be an absolute chaos and shambles before peace comes. The peace that is arrived at may be no more than an armed truce. But even then men will have to begin again to rebuild, and it will only add to the destruction if the spirits and the minds of those not directly involved become a chaos and a shambles now. The methods of free inquiry and enlightened co-operative effort have been interrupted before. It would be foolish to the point of criminality to stifle them deliberately at a time when they are most threatened.

What holds true of the more directly scientific methods of social control holds true in equal, perhaps in greater, measure for those concerns that seem (but only superficially) the luxuries of the spirit. It is a striking historical fact that some of the quiet, powerful creations of the human race, works that have left their permanent liberating influence on mankind, were produced by men far from insensitive to the miseries of mankind, in times of apparent and of real dissolution and untold hurt to the bodies and souls of some of the best of their generation. Even in times of peace there is every temptation to be distracted and to let the noise of events

54

in their hectic timeliness divert us from the arduous concerns of art and mind. It would do all of us some good in our hopeless moments of nihilism to recall what Pericles, according to Thucydides, said in the funeral oration over the bodies of those who had fallen in the war.

'Our constitution does not copy the laws of neighbouring states; we are rather a pattern to others than imitators ourselves. Its administration favours the many instead of the few; this is why it is called a democracy. If we look to the laws, they afford equal justice to all in their private differences; if to social standing, advancement in public life falls to reputation for capacity, class considerations not being allowed to interfere with merit; nor again does poverty bar the way; if a man is able to serve the state, he is not hindered by the obscurity of his condition. The freedom which we enjoy in our government extends also to our ordinary life. . . .

'Further, we provide plenty of means for the mind to refresh itself from business. We celebrate games and sacrifices all the year round, and the elegance of our private establishments forms a daily source of pleasure and helps to banish the spleen; while the magnitude of our city draws the produce of the world into our harbour, so that to the Athenian the fruits of other countries are as familiar a luxury as those of his own. . . .

'Nor are these the only points in which our city is worthy of admiration. We cultivate refinement without extravagance and knowledge without effeminacy; wealth we employ more for use than for show. . . .

'In short, I say that as a city we are the school of Hellas; while I doubt if the world can produce a man, who, where he has only himself to depend upon, is equal to so many emergencies, and graced by so happy a versatility as the Athenian. . . .' It was not of desolation or of misery that he spoke, but of what Athens at its best meant.

If we cease to keep alive the things that are civilized in our society, our land is destroyed without a bomb bursting or an invader landing on our shores. There would not be much point in defending a civilization in which every civilized interest had lapsed. The arts and our intellectual activities need to be kept alive, not simply because, when they are most eloquent, clear, and free, they are the concentration of our best energies and of ourselves, but also because they are liberators and nourishers of life. It is true that, as Spinoza pointed out, the conditions of civil liberty are necessary to the preserving of intellectual freedom. But important also is the maintenance of the habit and the work of free speculation (free even from responsibility to the urgencies of the moment), for ideas permeate the atmosphere in which freedom is cherished. The arts and thinking become more sombre and responsible and serious in a tragic time. They may seem irrelevant, but, paradoxically enough, their business becomes peculiarly urgent: to keep alive freedom and a deeper liberty, the play of mind and heart and imagination, in the living variety of human experience. Plato's *Republic*, Spinoza's *Ethics*, Dante's *Divine*

Comedy, and Wordsworth's *Prelude* were not written when the world was quietly happy. Their pages outlived the troubled eras in which their authors lived, and have brought light and healing to men in other troubled eras. Creative art and creative thought are life-continuing and life-renewing beyond the immediate clamour, even while destruction is rampant. And their creation may renew life for generations knowing happier times or facing other perils. Out of tragedy, thinking may envisage a way to lessen the tragedy of other generations, or make images of a way of life less disastrous than our own.

★

If we have been too hasty about science and its failure, we have been too hasty also in our assumption that democracy is ended because in certain parts of the world it is being flouted and discredited, because in the homes of such democracy as has existed in Western civilization the very processes of democracy have for long been confused and are now grimly interrupted. The democratic processes are very recent and have been very limited. There is even some responsible opinion among historians that they were never really alive and functioning in Germany and Italy of the nineteenth century. There has been increasing realization of this, and one has but to read for illustration the comments of the Labour Opposition in the British Parliament to know how little democracy has been operative in England. In the nineteenth century, even so wise an observer as John Stuart Mill assumed that the form of representative government itself would be enough. Ballot boxes and literacy were supposed to do the trick. We know very much better now. Jacques Barzun, in his recent illuminating book *Of Human Freedom*, has pointed out suggestively, as John Dewey in other terms has been pointing out these many years, that unless democracy — the flexible and courageous use of co-operative intelligence — functions throughout our lives it does not function at all. If it has failed, it has failed because it has been tried in such limited terms, because so much of privilege has prevented it from being tried further, because so much of life for so many people has been excluded. The snob has functioned in the arts and made them trivial and unintelligible, those very arts which might be the means of imaginative sharing of the whole of experience by all men, the means of utterance of what mattered most to them, and the images of a more vital and ordered condition of life. Democracy has not been tried in industry because special privilege has determined it should not be tried. It has not been tried in education because authority and tradition, the social deposit of habit, have continued to function there, and because groups — dominant for whatever reason — have wished to pass on inherited formulas rather than equip the young to develop fresh forms of living appropriate to new needs.

The democracies have failed in Europe, we hear, meaning by democracy the pluto-oligarchy that has continued through constitutional forms. What makes us so certain that it could not function if it were tried? Probably three things: lack of faith in the common man, lack of belief that people could be deeply or effectively concerned with the common good, and, third, a sense that society could not be effectively planned without suppressing the liberty of individual living.

There is nothing in the crescendo of evil that has swept over the Western world that ought to make us lose faith in the common man. It is curious how the waves of political methods and ideologies pass over the lives of ordinary people. Even today there is no reason to believe that the common man in the countries that we feel have betrayed the democratic ideal is so common, so brutal, or so vulgar as his leaders. Today, right now in Germany and, as the writer knows from personal experience, in Italy after fifteen years of a totalitarian régime, the plain people wish to live a simple human life. And even without education, with pitiful means and under brutal suppressions, the Italian peasant leads his life with a gay and human distinction.

God must have loved the common people, Lincoln remarked in an often-quoted utterance, because he made so many of them. The democratic hypothesis is simply that, given a chance, the common man may be a high, not a low, common denominator. For what we call the needs of the average man are those of everyone. He desires to eat, to sleep, to love. There is nothing that has happened to make us believe that those elements of decency and kindness, of living and letting live, which people exhibit if they are allowed to live without fear and insecurity, might not animate the decisions of mankind. We have not seriously tried to give the common man an adequate voice in the commonweal. It is the leaders of the democracies, not themselves democrats or brought up on a genuinely democratic concern, who have been complicitly instrumental in getting Europe into its present state. It is true now, possibly more than ever, that the generality of mankind, left to themselves, would live in amity and kindness. It is as much a challenge as ever to work for conditions of life under which people could come to be themselves, rather than to be stereotypes, or the victims of over-privilege, which makes them callous, or under-privilege, which makes them slaves. Men and women are not angels, but they are not devils either. They are men and women. The experiment is young yet, that of arranging the conditions of life so that men and women can quietly be themselves and live decently shared lives. The community feeling in any village in Vermont, even the help and kindliness in a slum in London or New York, has shown what can be done in that direction. The battle against entrenched privilege, against authoritarianism, against snobbishness of race or caste, has been steadily going on. It is a battle quite as important in the long run as that in China or in Europe. Only when that subtler battle is successful will the bloodier battles disappear.

It is still argued in many quarters that private pleasures, private greeds, and private interests will prevent that co-operative concern for the common good which is most people's business. The average man, we are told, is too engrossed in his own little concerns, the great leaders too preoccupied by vast privileges and interests, to be occupied with the common good. I think this is largely because the common good has been conceived of as an abstraction. The common good is the good of each. But has not the war, have not totalitarian régimes, shown that a common concern, or what is pictured as being so, may be everyone's concern? Nor need private interests be sacrificed for it. It is possible, with proper education, to promote a moral equivalent for war. And many are discovering how thin are the private interests which are not shared. They have a tincture of poison in them. It is hard to realize how much moral loneliness and spiritual isolation there is in a society where people have no roots, no common bonds, no comradely concerns.

But suppose we put the worst face on it. Suppose we say that the hope for human

nature, for scientific control, for co-operative sharing is not justified. As a matter of
fact it is our only hope, for until the method
of science and the organization of good
will are made effective, we shall be paying
in blood and in chaos as we have paid
these tragic years. But suppose we grant
that we are at the fatal turn, that every
generous human hope is rendered nil. Is
there anything else? There is — the present
and the eternal. Bad as the present is, it is
a good, as any future good must, in time,
be a present, too. Whatever good it has is
really good, just as good as it would be in
a better time. Transitory, too, as the
present is, it exhibits, as any present would,
the eternal. And in the recognition of
those present goods and manifestations of
the eternal (for the eternal is always the
same) lies a hint of what refuge we still
have, if all our hopes founder.

★

It may seem strange to the point of per-
versity to declare in an almost immitigably

tragic time that a vivid sense of the present is one of the best antidotes to despair. But the fact is, so great is the impact of events upon us, that we are losing the capacity to realize the present at all. Even in quiet times most people live for the most part at second-hand, by labels and clichés passing for experience. In tense periods such as that through which we are passing, we do not so much live as we are interrupted in living by dire intimations, by signals of death and darkness. We do not experience the present at all as a poet or any free spirit or, in a word, any person completely alive feels it. Each moment is filled with such complex uncertainty that we are losing the capacity to take or to feel the moment as it is in itself — now. Haunted habitually by the thought of how all goods are threatened, we no longer have the freedom of spirit to be wholly or whole-heartedly acquainted with such goods of life as even now there are, such goods of life as persist, whatever ardours and endurances face men. These we experience at their fullest in art and play, in friendship and affection, or in our work (if we happen to be lucky), and in all those activities which release and enhance the sense of being and, with it, the sense of joy.

It seems more than perverse, it would appear gratuitous, to remind us to live in the present, which we think is all too palpably with us. But is it? Even to the chaos and the misery of it we become numbed. A battleship is destroyed, and we glibly speak of the loss of a thousand men. But we do not 'realize' in imagination the drowning of a single man or the sorrow of those who loved him. Men huddled on the Western Front become a line in a communiqué, a sentence in a strategical plan. One cannot help reflecting how much of human misery might have been, may still be, averted if it should become a habit of mankind to see in images of first-hand joy or sorrow what would be the consequences of a crusade upon which it is asked to engage or a fanaticism to which it is already committed. What will some hoped-for future *look* like, *feel* like, *be* like, when it becomes a present, in all its urgency of glow or lethargy, pleasure or pain? There ought to be a poet or a painter in the employ of every moralist or Utopian, to present him with a picture, unmistakable in its edge and vividness, of what the engineered or prescribed happiness for which he is battling would be to the mind and the senses and the heart of men when it actually ceased to be a blueprint and became a daily human fact to sense and feeling.

But if men forget that the future will some day be a present, they forget, too, that the present is already here, and that even in a dark time some of the brightness for which they long is open to the responsive senses, the welcoming heart, and the liberated mind. The moments as they pass even now have their tang and character. They may yield even now the contagious joy of feeling and perception. Here are the familiar flowers, the music we love, the poetry by which we are moved. Here are the books and companions, the ideas and the relaxations, the gaieties and the co-operative tasks of our familiar world. These things may be threatened, they may be precarious, they may be ours only by the grace of God, or of geographical or economic accident. But undeniably, beckoningly, along with the portents and alarms, here they are. Here, in all tragic times, they always have been, affording challenge and delight to the senses, solace and nourishment for the affections, and friendly stimulus to the understanding.

Why should we feel that they are any less good, any less creditable, than in the past?

The days that make us happy make us
    wise,

John Masefield once wrote. They are instructions, by admirable instance, of what elements would go into a happy society. They are the first-hand realization of the extent to which civilization has achieved anything more than an abstract boast. That distant promised world of felicity — which we now find it so hard to believe in — what would it be in its eventual bright day but a bright day come to actuality for all mankind in the first-hand happiness men and women would experience in an eventual here and now?

The moments of happiness possible to us even now are a more real consolation, perhaps, than any promise of future happiness would be, and not simply because they are birds in the hand. They are the evidences and tokens of a better world. If that better world is impossible, at least now we have glimpses of what in any case it would have been or would have resembled. If a better world is still possible, what better clues could we have to what it would be, or what we should work for it to be, than these direct felicities, needing no argument or proof, that we now know? These little islands of sound life in a sick world, do they not lend some colour to our hopes of a happier time, do they not suggest what the colour of such a happier time would be? A better world seems a little less impossible if a little of its good, even in the midst of tragedy, shines through the tragedy now. Is it not part of the tragedy of our time, not that remote goods are being made remoter, but that actual good is being suspended? The hints of a better order are because of this very fact being stilled.

What better planned economy of human hope could there be than one that took as its criteria such elements of delight and friendliness, and rationality, as are possible to the fortunate and, at moments, to the unfortunate, even now? These are paragraphs of the good life, tinctured only by the sense that such good fortune is very rare and that they are so scattered, so precarious, and that there is so little companionship in them. The awareness of these present paragraphs of the good life can be enhanced through education in the arts. Companionship in them can be increased through the still possible art of friendship even in an all-hating world. Education in delight and in the sharing of delight may be not only an antidote to the poison of despair. If made sufficiently contagious as an attitude toward life, it may be an instrument for removing the grounds for despair. If we learn now to see what the goods of life are and how they gain by being shared, the infinite possibilities of human intelligence and natural resources in the world may be organized for the common good. In the broad sense the arts will be an education in feeling, and the art of politics will be human friendship made a standard political practice.

Nor need there be any fear, I think, that the planning of the instruments of living in the interests of human happiness will be an enemy of human liberty. Planning the condition by which human beings can live at all and live together does not mean prescribing what that particular kind of happiness will be. The vaunted liberties of a democratic society have been too often the liberties of the already entrenched and privileged, the economic and moral slavery of the many. To organize the means of living for all is not to preclude the possibility of living well, or variously or individually, by each. To make and secure life for all is not to destroy liberty and happiness for each; it is to promote them. Only where 'planning' becomes an end in itself, and the individual is a cog in a totalitarian machine, does organization by intelligence mean discipline by force.

A sense of the present thus has an important moral bearing, one might almost say a moral exaltation. A paradise on earth may not be impossible, for any such heaven would be composed of colours and joys and companionships such as we now in the worst of times have still been able to know. All the more reason to find the wit and the will to build a society in which these can be more generally and generously pervasive. We need not fear that human nature is incapable of such realization, for human nature is largely what its opportunities and circumstances make it. And even where its opportunities and circumstances have been extremely limited, it has broken through to heights of joy and accomplishment that should make us modify our suspicion that only cruelty and barbarism are in its heart. The history of civilization may be looked at as the history of selfishness and cruelty. But that history is the history also of saints, artists, and mystics. It ought not to be too much to believe, in the midst of disaster, that mankind can invent the conditions of human happiness, that mankind whose geniuses have invented and imagined so much, and whose simple people have enjoyed so much, under difficulty. And it is well to be reminded that such happiness is not impossible, for in the midst of violence and stupidity it has been achieved in the past; though clouded, it is being experienced fitfully even now.

★

But suppose not. Suppose we take the worst alternative. The most desperate doubt at least or at last renders us free men. It liberates us at once from hope and fear. It is not cynical but realistic to say that the first condition of serenity is not to have too great expectations; it is essential, if we are to have peace of mind in times of crisis, that we have no expectations at all.

Nor is this impossible. The life of even the most fortunate individual, the history of even the most tranquil society, is marked at any moment by doubts, anxieties, hopes, fears, expectations, and regrets. The crisis of civilization through which we are living is, though a tragic moment, a moment only in the history of the cosmos, an episode only in the history of men. History moves in long waves; we are caught in the roughest surf today, and hurled about by it. But in the midst of the ocean it will be calm tomorrow. In its depths it is calm today. Men have learned, though it requires genius of both ardour and disinterestedness to learn it, to look upon the worst with equanimity.

There are moments of individual lives when we are enabled, for the time being,

if only for the time being, to survey existence in its own terms and detach it and
ourselves from the jaws of hoped or feared
futurity. Great tragic art enables us to do
that. It is a familiar fact that tragedy
quiets and elevates rather than distracts
and destroys us. If happiness must eventu-
ally be a here and now, even in the
pleasantest lives and the most genial
societies frustration is almost universal,
and death, the final frustration for every
living creature, for any way of life, is
inevitable. The present is always with us,
in the most desperate of times. The eternal
is always illustrated, sometimes tragically
illustrated, in even the most felicitous
present. To discipline ourselves to live
without hope or expectation does not
mean that we pass to hopelessness and
despair. It means, quite the contrary, that
we pass to genuine serenity. To discover
that our lives are doomed even in times of
peace, that civilization as we now know it
may be doomed in times of war, is to meet
experience in its most direct and candid
terms. It is to live in the immediate for

whatever beauty it may incarnate, truth it may reveal, or good it may enshrine. But such beauties, goods, and truths encountered will be an initiation to eternity, even to a mortal and doomed creature in a society whose most generous hopes are cancelled.

The eternal we have always with us and it is always at once a stimulant and an anodyne. Everyone recalls the preternatural lucidity of an autumn day, when every colour, so soon to fade utterly, has for the moment the quality of timeless being. 'The spirit lives in this continual sense of the ultimate in the immediate.' To behold the recurrent types of energy and the spending of energy, of life and the passing of life, of hope and the disillusion that follows upon it, such beholding may — even if the energy, life, and hope be our own — raise us from the hurt and risk incident to existence in time to the peace of the eternal. To experience eternity does not take a long time. It may take an instant, as in the presence of a great work of art where the greatest number of energies are focused in the most intense concentration. On any basis of what we might wish existence to be, the prospects of our time may be very sad indeed. But would not the most peaceful society and the most secure material existence, the gayest association, have their inner voice of disillusion and disappointment, too? Does not even ecstasy of love or art borrow part of its poignancy from the hushed obbligato of fatality that hovers over it, the inner voice of futility that whispers in it? The death's head at the banquet is a grim but true image for the most radiantly happy life. But experience has half its venom removed when it is held at arm's length, with the detachment of contemplation. The crucial state of civilization at the present juncture has simply dramatized on a colossal scale the anxiety and indecision that cloud even the most auspicious turns of individual lives or the lives of nations and cultures. Life is always at some turning point. Great poets and seers have taught us in the past, they may teach us now, to behold the view. Stopping thus to behold it, its urgency, though not its tragedy, may be removed. And then we shall be enabled to behold what men have always beheld when they have raised their eyes to see: the serene, unending recurrences in Nature, the eternal forms and types of happiness and suffering, of cruelty and wisdom, of barbarism and saintliness, that perpetually return on the human scene. Even if our worst fears are realized, Nature will still breathe easily, and generate new men in new times to have hopes and fears again. While we live, at least, we can be alive in the perpetual music of the dream, the eternal note of the tragedy. And it is no small consolation to know, among these recurrences so regular as to be a kind of eternity, 'the beginning, if not the fullness of beauty'. That is something to have lived for, to live by, when all else fails.

If all else fails! One of the advantages of detachment is that it makes us see how hasty our despairs have been, how provincial, even on the human scale, our assumption of tragedy. The darkness now seems absolute. Men before us have forgotten that it hides the morning star.